A Song in Amber

the poetry of
CRAIG WILLIAM ANDREWS

A Song in Amber

An effulgent publication of
AUTUMN SUN PUBLISHING
Sequim, Washington

A Song in Amber
by Craig William Andrews

Copyright © 2014 by Craig William Andrews
All rights reserved.
Printed in the United States of America

Published by
Craig Andrews / Autumn Sun Publishing
tarasparkman@yahoo.com

Typestyle: Sabon
Book Design by Ruth Marcus, Rmarcus@olypen.com

No part of this book may be used or reproduced in any manner whatsoever without the written permission of the author.

ISBN 978-0692263-63-1

A Song in Amber

Being a poem in twelve parts
Written in reverence
for the deep yin foundation
Spirit of this World

Theme

May each word lie precisely where it must
And not one syllable be lost
To wander where it does not belong

Preface

And so I have taken out a rag and wiped the
  small table clean of dust
Where I shall place this manuscript while I
  nurture it
While it grows
On the table next to my big chair
Where I sometimes sleep
And dream of strange lands
Or in the stillness before dawn
When the world is wrapped in slumber
I deftly imagine myself to be the sire of some
  deeply infectious Beauty which starts small
But speeds from Soul to Soul
Changing the landscape in sublimely Mystical
  Ways
Bringing us all into the land of our Dreaming
Where all people live blessed
With Perfect Vision
With Divine Love,
And my glance falls upon the notebook which
  lays upon the table
And I play the theme back within my mind
"May each word lie precisely where it must
And not one syllable be lost

To wander where it does not belong,"
For the Quality of the Enchantment rests
   within the purity of the Heart
The purity of the thought;
The skill and the patience of the crafting.

A Song in Amber

Canto 1

I Am a River
Which flows into your sea

As I unfold in You
So you unfold in Me

Canto II

Do you see that I am constantly dying for the
   sake of what is birthing forth?
The Temple you have built for Me will one
   day turn into dust
Will you build a new one
As the Tree births the Tree?
Or will you find Me within the Temple
   of your Heart
Opening a new door into the Blossoming
   of My Song.

Canto III

I Am the deer
Which silently crosses your Path
In Golden Faerie Light

I Am the Bird
Which flies across the face of the Moon in Twilight
Tracing the Starlight Pentagram
Upon the Matrix of Silver Enchantment,

I Am the scent of Orange blossoms
On the Breath of a warm Summer's night
And the dancing diamond light upon the Sea,
Turn to Me
I will be these things to you,

Hold Me
I will Breathe through you,
Love Me
I will rise up through you
As Sunlight through dell and glen
As life-blood
Into the highest leaf of my Sacred Elm.

Canto IV

I Am the Bird
Which flys across the darkening sky
Have you not seen me?
I Am flying back to the Ancient Temple,
I will walk in Her Moonlit Gardens
I will rest in Her Dream until Morning,
I have not forgotten the way Home.

Canto V

It has been raining for days and days,
The tall Cedar and Fir are wearing clouds,
The clouds are forested
Impregnated with the misty shadow of possibility,
With a Presence which drifts back Forever
Into moss and rock and dripping earth,
And into my cells
Which swim in the memory of Water,
For Water is Her Ancient Home.

Canto VI

It is the sense of something "Other"
Which leads the Pilgrim on,
That Life shall not be a tune
Which endlessly circles about its own refrain,
But a Symphony which constantly births
Into the Spiral of Presents Becoming,

Never to Return

Nor is the Past some imagined line
Which endlessly stretches down musty corridors
To echo through cobwebbed rooms
Devoid of dance and laughter,
But rather an ever expanding and deepening
Of this one moment of birthing awareness,
This only time of Being,
For you see,
The Pilgrims eyes are focused upon the Promise,
The first Covenant between the Universal Way
And the Blossoming of the Earth,
That She shall rise upon the Wings of Her
   Enchantment
And Wonder shall be Her Gift
To every Mother's Child.

Canto VII

Do you see? My friend,
How we are dancing through each other as
    doorways,
Set into each other as perfect mirrors,
Reflecting and experiencing through endless Realms,

And our eyes,
Each to other,
Windows through which Nature seeks Her Self
In Her Quest for a true Kindness,

Do you see the Heart which we hold in the palms of
    our hands,
Breathing "Yes!"
Into our Past of confusion and pain,
We choose to Love.

Canto VIII

I have walked,
For miles and miles,
Listening to the crunch of the stones
Beneath my feet;

Walked,
Through the cool damp of the early morning light,
Through the rising heat of the day,
Into the furnace of afternoon,
Into the soft breeze of evening;

I have Walked forever
Just to see one small flower,
Just to look, as a bird would look,
Over rivers, and mountains, and towns;

I have Walked,
Or my body has Walked,
Or my Heart,
Or my Mind,
Those things which I do not understand;

Or I have lifted my feet
While the Earth has turned beneath me;
A captured Spark of Soul

Watching the panorama of Life
Played upon the Silver Screen of Eternity;

I have Walked,
And seen the dusty lifetimes of some imagined past
Turn into the days and nights
Of some lofty Mystery,
Some greater journey which plays itself in light and shadow

Loves and passions,
Deaths and Births, and quiet still moments
Of All Knowing Illumination;

I have Walked,
And seen those who have walked beside me,
And felt those who have walked through me,
Brothers and Sisters on the same Dharma Road,
Sharing Life
As the leaves of the Tree share the Wind.

Canto IX

On a Winter Solstice Morning
The sky was draped in Cloud Magic
While the mist wove a Chinese Tapestry
In amongst the Redwood forest ridges
A rebirth into the Wonder and the Mystery
Which form the Natural Womb of Life
And I said to My Self,
"Ah!" This is very good indeed!

Canto X

There is a Prophecy proclaimed in Light
Whispered amongst the Nations of the Stars,
Foretold on the Tapestry
Which hangs in the Universal Hall,
A Prophecy danced in the Moonlight
To fiddles and pipes,
Hissed by the wind through the long dry grass,
Between the river in the sun
And the shady forest grove,
A Prophecy foretold in the chirp of the Robin
And the call of the Wren,

For just as all the Planets have Souls
So the Earth shall Awake!
Perhaps on a Summer's Solstice Morning
With the Dawning of the Day.

Canto XI

In the very start of morning,
In the very first light of day,
There is a hush,
A stillness which holds all things,
And this is a very Sacred Time
Which is only broken by the first song of a bird,

In the beginning of the dawn,
One bird is chosen to call forth the birthing of
    the day
That the Silvered Symphony of Creation
Begins with one small chirp,
For this is the Natural Way,
And this is a very beautiful thing
Which resonates within the Heart
And soothes the urgency of our Being.

Canto XII

There is a Wisdom
Which tells of Souls Endless Flight
Through forever becoming spirals
Of moments unfolding dance,

A Wisdom
Which lightly walks the web
Of minds transcendental knowledge,
And feels through the Ageless Path
Of Breath's dawning vision of Transformation
Into Worlds yet to Become,

A Wisdom which shimmers about the
Highest buds of Summer's leaves
And flows in golden stream
Through the twigs, branches, and trunk
Of Life's Sacred Tree

A Wisdom which drinks of Her Spring
In the Hallowed Grove of Her Dream

Which circles its Women about the Moon,
And its Men about its Women,
Whispers in the language of wind and leaves,

Shouts in the opening of blossoms,
And laughs in the play of lightly falling rain

And for this Wisdom no school is built
No lineage is defended
Or great serious consideration given
To the relative value of Sacred Names

For this Wisdom no tax is levied,
And no army be trained

No man,
And no Woman,
Need work in factories drear
Until they are too weary to lift their voices in song,
And no child need cry
For want of Life's abundance

For this Wisdom is Her Wisdom,
Whose dream is Ecstasy,
Unending celebration of Life,
And Endless flow into Wonder,

Which unlike the marshaled cadence chant
Before the walls of Jericho,
Shall see the great seriousness of this world
Crumble before the smiling
Clear waters of Her Heart.

Fly, My brave young Eagle/Song of My Heart
And when you return
Enfold about me
The wings of a Swan

OTHER BOOKS
BY
CRAIG WILLIAM ANDREWS

Acts of Creation

Some Things Gentle
Some Things Kind

www.ingramcontent.com/pod-product-compliance
Lightning Source LLC
Chambersburg PA
CBHW031943070426
42450CB00006BA/869